Tricky Puzzles

for clever kids

Isabella
Riedler

Sterling Publishing Co., Inc.
New York

10 9 8 7 6 5 4 3 2 1

Published by Sterling Publishing Company, Inc.
387 Park Avenue South, New York, N.Y. 10016
Originally published under the title *Ratsel Rakete* and © 1999
by Arena Verlag GmbH, Wurzburg, Germany
English transkation © 2001 by Sterling Publishing
Distributed in Canada by Sterling Publishing
c/o Canadian Manda Group, One Atlantic Avenue, Suite 105
Toronto, Ontario, Canada M6K 3E7
Distributed in Great Britain and Europe by Chris Lloyd at Orca Book
Services, Stanley House, Fleets Lane, Poole BH15 3AJ, England
Distributed in Australia by Capricorn Link (Australia) Pty Ltd.
P.O. Box 704, Windsor, NSW 2756 Australia

Sterling ISBN 0-8069-6753-6

1. Swimming Marathon

All swimmers are swimming to the right—except one!
Can you find her?

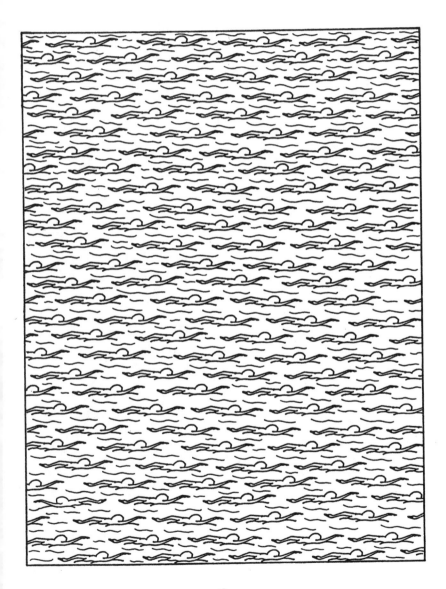

2. Down the Slide

In each picture, 3 children are going down the slide. If you look carefully, you'll see that there are only 8 different

children and you are seeing each one 3 times. Can you find each "triplet"?

3. A Huge Hole

It was spring when Richard took his tent out of the closet
and set it up. He was shocked to see that moths had eaten
a huge hole out of it during the winter.

How many boxes did the moths eat?

4. Where Is My Wife?

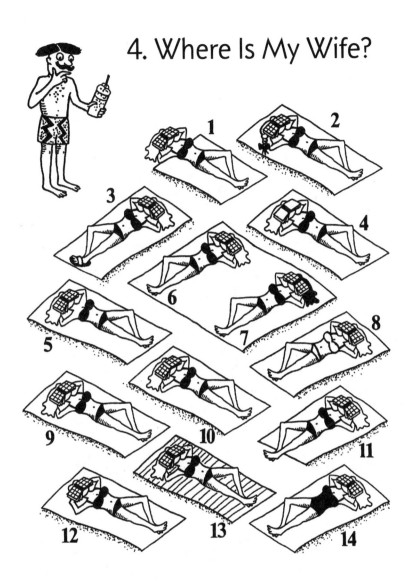

Her black bikini has straps. The book she is reading has a black back and a checkerboard cover. Her hair is light and long. She is lying all by herself on a towel that is white and longer than she is tall. She is barefoot.

Which one is she?

5. Who Is Flying Where?

The 3 planes below are flying to 3 different cities. Where is each one landing?

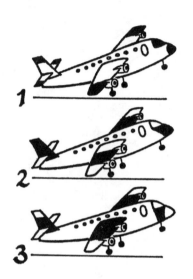

1 _____

2 _____

3 _____

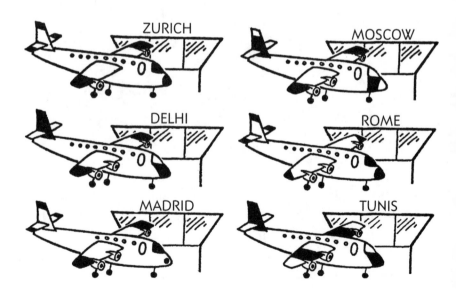

ZURICH

MOSCOW

DELHI

ROME

MADRID

TUNIS

9

6. Long Tongues

Which chameleon is licking the ice cream cone?

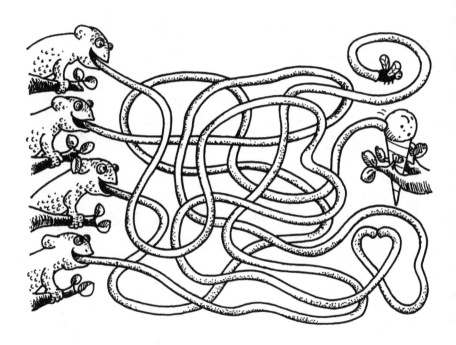

7. Looking for the Boomerang

Tom's boomerang is stuck between the clothes hangers. Will you help him find it?

8. Who Is Serving the Coffee?

Connect the dots to find out.

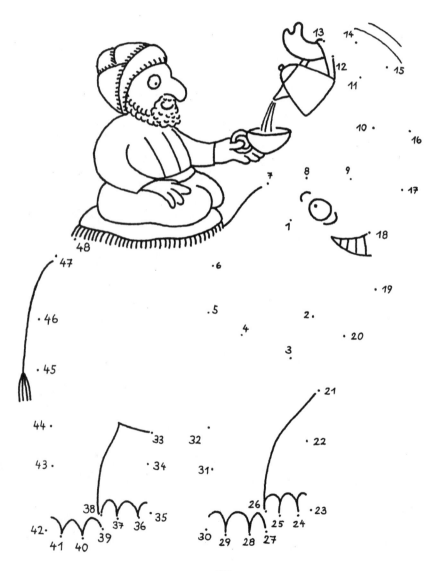

9. On a Gondola in Venice

Which canal will get the gondola to the palace?

10. Kite Festival

The owners have written numbers from 1 to 9 on the kites below. When you add up the numbers that appear on each kite and then compare the totals, you'll know which kite is flying on the longest string.

11. Four Triplets

There are 4 triplets in this group of 12 cats. Can you find them? If you want to check your answer, the numbers of each set of triplets will always add up to 30.

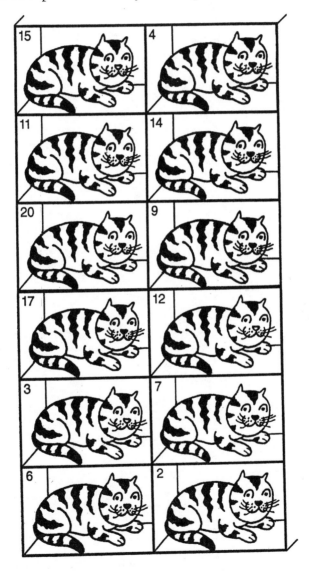

12. Camels

Can you find the complete camel?

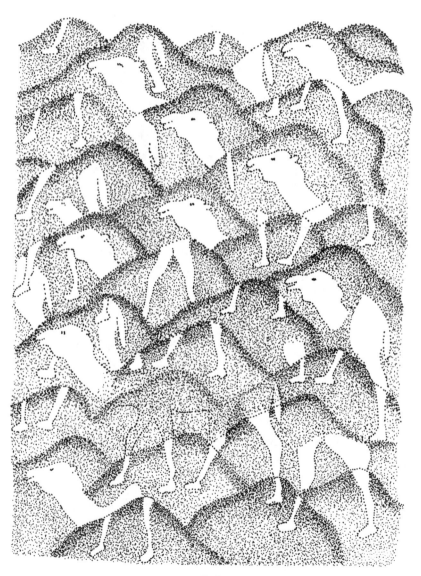

13. Wild River

Hubert lost his paddle going down the river in his kayak.
Where is it?

14. Half a Crown

Show the king which 1 of the 4 parts will complete his crown perfectly.

15. New Eyeglasses

Which 2 of these 17 lenses can the owl insert into its frame, so that it can see just as well with both eyes? The same mouse has to appear in both lenses.

16. Hat Heaven

A strong wind blew the chef's hat into the clouds. Where is it?

17. Wash Day

Find 7 differences between these 2 pictures before the laundry dries!

18. Mysterious Request

The passenger in this taxi will not tell the driver her destination. Instead, she says:

"Go straight for a few blocks. Then make a left twice, then a right twice, then make a left and then a right and again a left."

Which house does the woman want to get to?

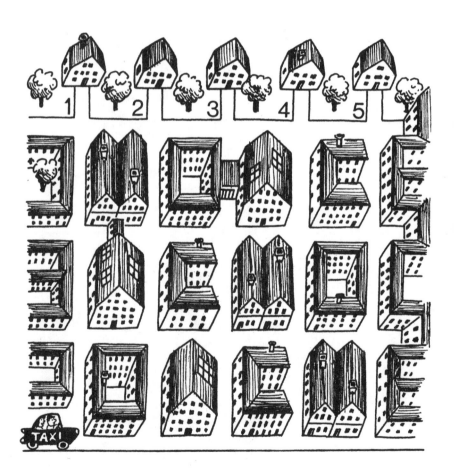

19. Rock Climbing

Can you find 15 differences in these 2 pictures—before the rock climber reaches the top of the mountain?

20. Greetings from the Woodchuck

Which of the 8 views through the telescope accurately shows the cute little woodchuck at the top of the mountain?

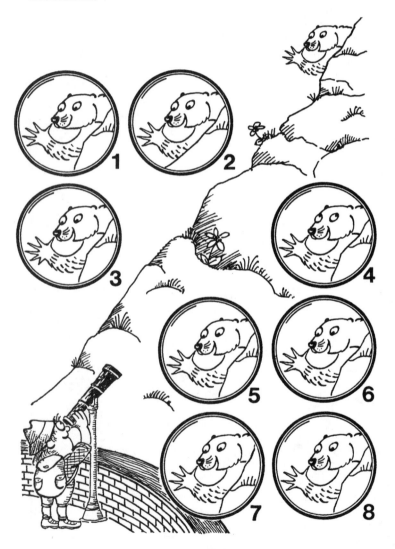

21. Where Is the  ?

22. How Old Is This Tree?

On this tree are numbers from 1 to 20. Wait a minute! Some of those numbers are missing! If you write the missing numbers into the row of boxes below and then add them up, the total that you get will tell you how old the tree is.

23. Which 6 Objects...

Which 6 objects do not appear twice?

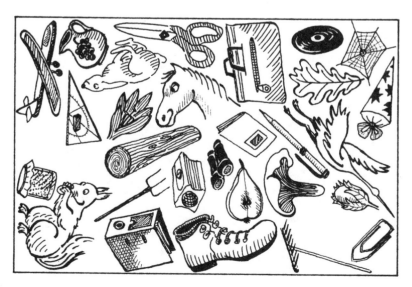

24. Hibernation

Which bear lives in this cave? To find out, compare the outlines of the bears with the outline at the entrance of the cave.

25. Gathering of the Ravens

Where are the 6 rooks among all these ravens? Rooks are birds that have a bare patch of skin at the base of their bills.

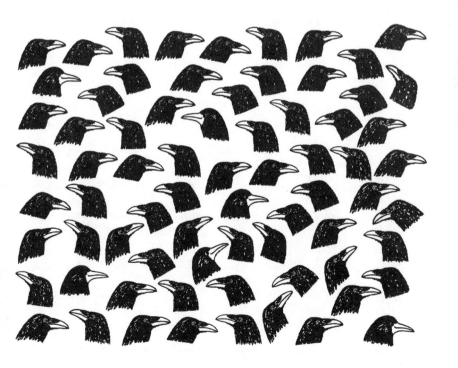

26. In the Hat Shop

In the picture on top, Billy is going into the shop to buy a new hat. He tries on all the hats and caps and puts them back in a different spot. He buys one of the hats, and the clerk replaces it with another hat. Which piece does Billy take with him and which one is new?

27. Looking for Footprints

The blackbird landed between the branches 3 times, leaving its footprints. Where are these spots?

28. Home of the Fountain Pen

Into which of the 4 cases does the fountain pen fit?

29. Crazy about Bookmarks

Is a bookmark sticking out of every page of these books? Not quite! Look in each book for the page that has no bookmark sticking out! If you cannot find it by just using your eyes, a ruler may help.

30. Gingerbread Dominoes

Charlie is supposed to play dominoes with these 9 ginger-breads, beginning with 6/6. If he can match up the pieces into a sequence so that just one remains, he is allowed to eat it. Which one will he get to eat?

31. Many Great-Smelling Gingerbreads

Can you find 4 cards (aces) and 3 dice hidden among these sweets?

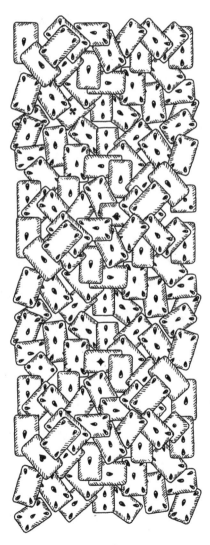

32. Hidden Gifts

Which of these 4 piles of gifts is Santa carrying under his hat?

33. From Fall to Winter

Put these New England pictures into the correct sequence, beginning with picture #2, and follow the seasons. Which picture does not fit?

34. Star Points

Monica made the stars in the left-hand picture herself, and the ones in the right picture were made by Mark. Who made the star with the fewest points and who made the one with the most points?

35. Where Is the Reindeer?

36. Self Service

Which bird picked up its package from which Santa Claus?

37. Decorating the Christmas Tree

Match up the Christmas ornaments on the left with those on the right. Also when you write the letters that are next to the ornaments (in the sequence 1 to 9), you'll find the name of one of the figures in most every nativity scene.

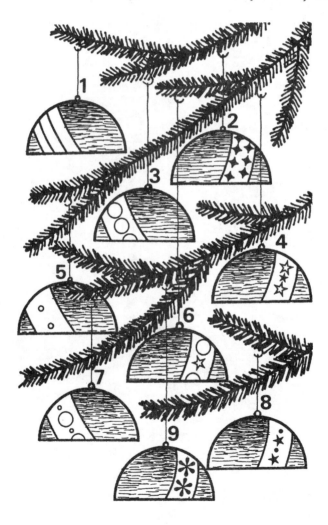

A T R A L H B A S

43

38. The Snowman's Hat

Which of the 15 pots is on the head of the snowman?

39. A Sweet Job

You are allowed to take 5 cookies from this plate, but only those whose numbers add up to 100.

Which 5 are those?

40. Cookie Dough

The cookies on the baking sheet (in the center) all come from one of these batches of dough. Which one?

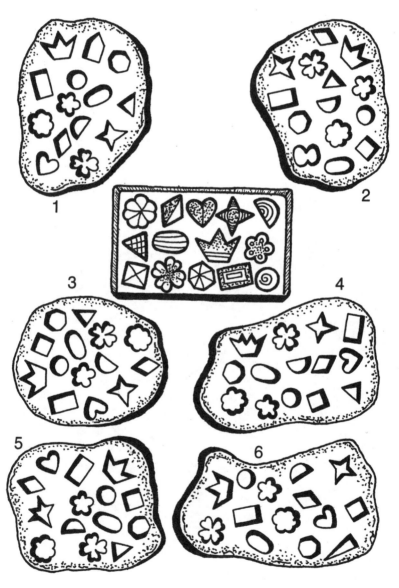

1

2

3

4

5

6

41. John's Christmas Wish

Which one of the 14 guitars is in the wrapped package?

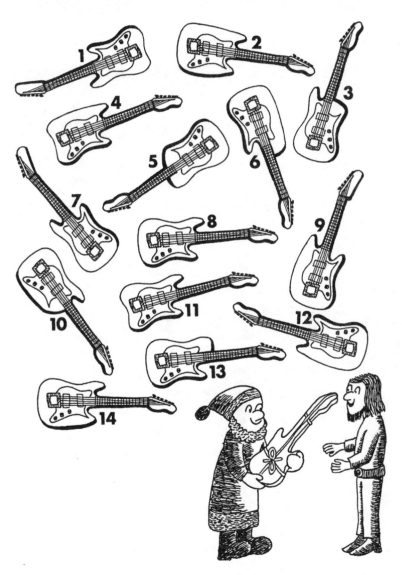

42. Amazing Violins

Snails have been used to create 3 of these violins! Which are they?

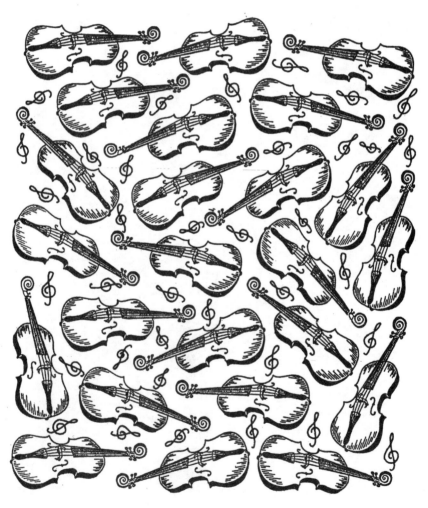

43. The Yawning Frog

Connect the dots and you'll find out whom the frog is watching.

44. The Leaping Seal

Which of the 4 seals has already jumped through the thin ice? Compare the heads and bodies of the seals with the shape that you see in the ice!

45. Four Skaters

Which 2 penguins skated the circles around the 2 seals?

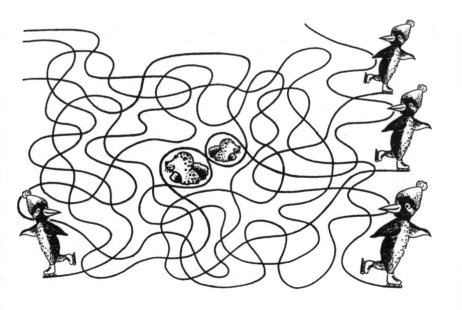

51

46. Skating Elks

Can you find 20 differences between these 2 pictures before one of the elks skids?

53

47. Identical Squares

As you see, the drawing of the large hockey-playing snowman (left) has been broken down into 40 squares. The drawing on the right has also been broken into squares—35 of them. In the 2 drawings, 3 of the boxes are exactly the same—although the sizes are different. Can you find these 3 pairs?

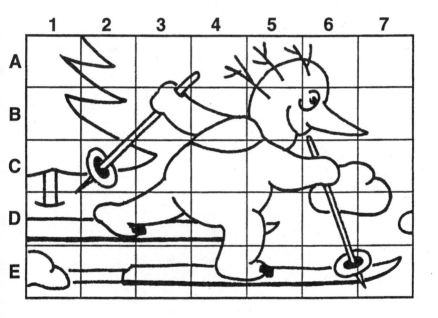

48. The Sled

Can you find 7 differences between the 2 pictures?

49. Tree Slalom

The trees on this course take the place of poles. From start to finish, the runners may only go around trees that are the same type as the ones at their starting-point. When you follow their tracks and try to connect them, you'll find out which is the only skier to run the slalom without making a mistake.

57

50. Who Shot the Goal?

51. What's the Game?

Connect the dots and you'll recognize a popular winter sport!

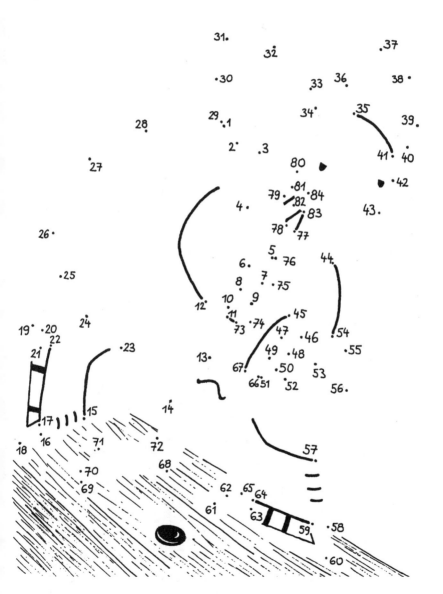

52. The Big Snowball Fight

There are 2 teams—one on the left, one on the right. The kids on the left throw snowballs at the kids on the right and vice versa. Find out which picture-pairs fit together and you'll know who hit whom!

GREG

PETER

EVE

BOB

SUSANNE

GEORGE

WILL

KEN

PHILIP

ALICE

HANNAH

PAUL

61

53. Downhill Skiers

Which of these "ski-bunnies" fit exactly into the outlines?

54. Let's Hit the Slopes

Normally, 1 person carries 1 pair of skies. But here, somewhere, 2 people together are carrying 1 pair. Where are those 2?

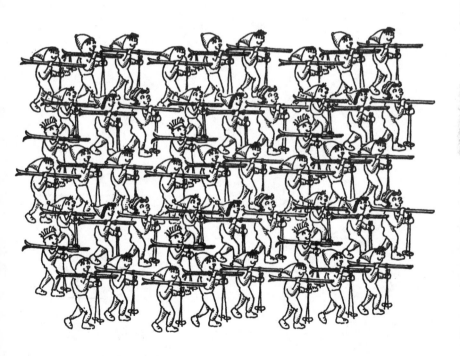

55. Six Snowballs

Roberto is rolling down the mountain in 1 of these 6 snowballs. Which one?

56. Snowman Mountain

How many snowmen can you build from all those spare
parts that make up the mountain? The fellow at the top is
your model and he doesn't count.

57. On the Track

When you connect the dots you'll know why the little bear is feeling so hot!

58. Bank Robbery

Can you find 15 differences between the 2 pictures—before the bank robber makes his getaway?

59. Potato Stamp

Mimi made this stamp out of a potato. On which of these 4 pieces of paper has Mimi put her stamp?

60. Carnival Game

Into which 4 holes do you have to throw a ball in order to score 60 points exactly?

61. RRRRocket

Among all those Rs, there are 5 other letters. When you find the letters, put them into the right sequence and you'll find the name of the planet to which the rocket is flying.

62. Lucky Hit

In the picture on top, 7 kids are throwing snowballs over the house. In the picture below, you see where they land. Who hit the person who is shoveling the snow?

63. On Top of the World

Connect the dots and you'll see who feels on top of the world.

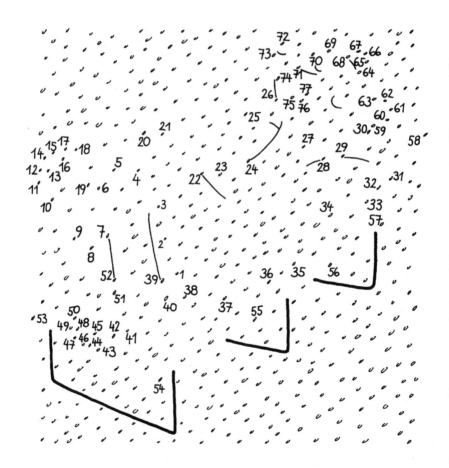

64. The Jester's Hat

Which of the 7 decorations is not on the jester's hat?

65. Where Is My Mask?

My mask has five pointy light-colored feathers. The mouth is open, the eyes are narrow, and there's a black spot on the nose. The beard does not have a black spot. The eyebrows are light-colored and the cheeks are dark.

66. Calculating with 2 Clowns

When you add up all the numbers in each clown, you'll find out the number of costume parties that each of them has attended during the last 10 years! (6 and 9 are not upside down).

67. The Russian Doll

Put a piece of tracing paper—or any paper you can see through—over the picture and draw the doll. Don't go over any line twice.

68. Three Faces

In the 2 pictures below, 3 faces do not appear in both pictures. Which 3?

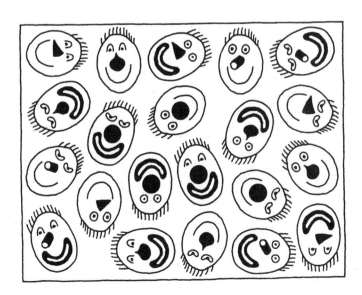

69. Butterflies

Which butterfly flew out of the flower?

70. Through the Hedge

Show the caterpillar the path through the hedge! It must not come out next to the bird, but on the left side of the hedge.

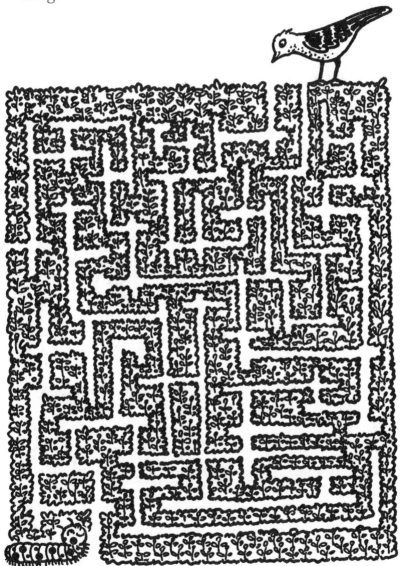

71. The Centipede

The centipede can show this number for only 7 minutes more. After that it will become too exhausting. Before that time, can you find 10 differences between the 2 pictures?

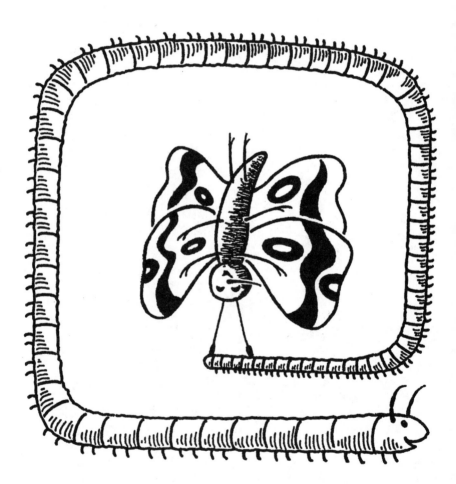

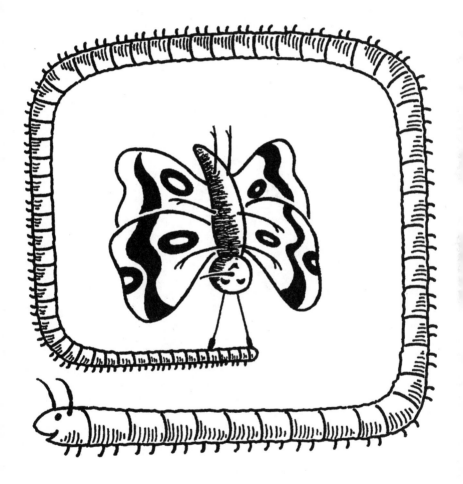

72. Egg Fraud

It looks as if all 18 animals hatched. But anyone who has some knowledge of zoology knows that only 3 of them hatch! Do you know this trio?

73. Rabbit Company

Can you find the 1 rabbit whose ear shape, whiskers, hind legs, and basket are not repeated in any of the other 6 rabbits?

74. Where Are the Rabbits?

Where are the 5 rabbits with 1 ear—and the 5 rabbits with 3 ears?

75. Painter and Model

Connect the dots and you'll find out what the rabbit has drawn.

76. Look for 15 differences!

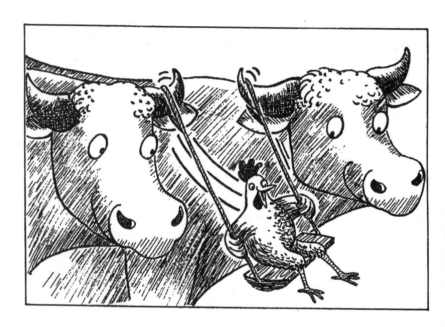

77. A Museum Piece

If you want to know how old this vase is, you need to add up all the numbers! (6 and 9 are not upside down).

78. Painting Easter Eggs

After these Easter eggs were decorated, these 4 kids added their own special designs to some of them. Paula painted her freckles, Jeff painted one of his buttons, David painted

DAVID

VICKIE

his eyeglasses, and Vickie painted the bow in her hair. The kids "signed" 12 eggs altogether. Can you find them—and tell how many eggs each kid signed?

79. The Giant Egg

An artist painted this egg beautifully. But when you look closely, you will see one pattern in each of the 8 rows that does not fit. Can you find these mistakes?

80. Frog Tuba

Which mouthpiece must the frog blow into so that a sound comes out of the funnel?

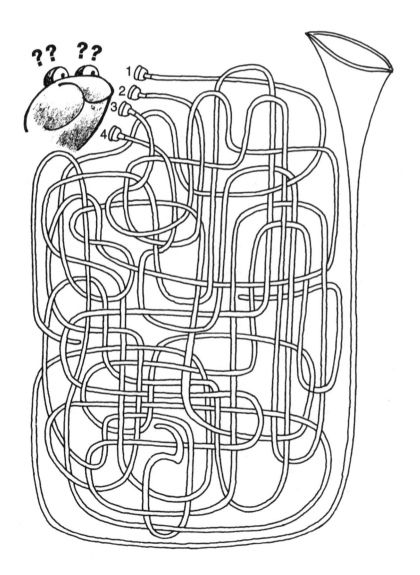

81. Who Is Riding?

When you connect the lines, which are interrupted by the bushes, you will see who is riding on whom!

82. Exchanging Ears

As you know, rabbits always have 2 identical ears, but obviously, the illustrator of this book has never seen a real rabbit. Can you find ears that match for each rabbit? (One letter and one number always go together.)

83. Who Is Older?

When you count all the numbers in these 2 steam engines, you'll find out which one is older. (9 and 6 are not upside down.)

84. Going Swimming

Which numbered section is missing in the picture at the top?

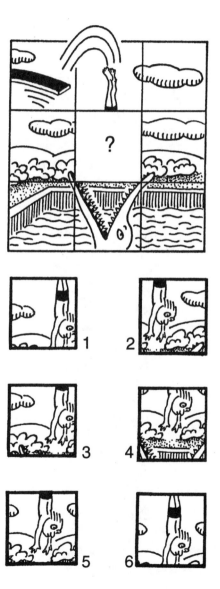

85. Crocodile in Love

With the help of the information in the bubble, can you discover the crocodile on the right side that is exactly what this romantic crocodile has in mind?

My dream partner must not have a gap in his teeth. His jaws must be the same length, and he mustn't be cross-eyed. His tail must be pointy, and I would love it if his forefoot had four claws!

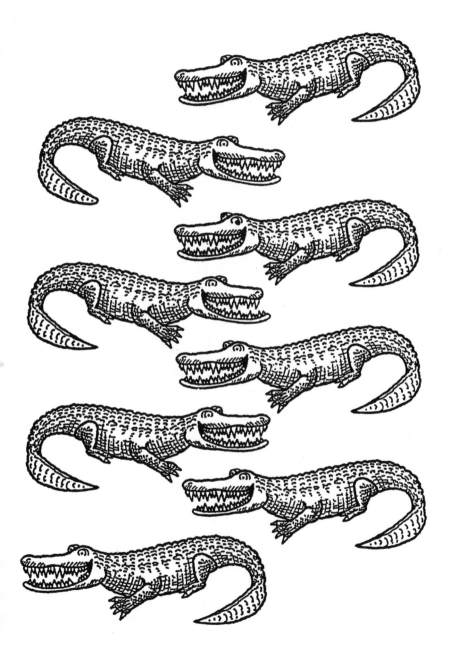

86. Crocodile Snack

Which crocodile bit into the sausage?

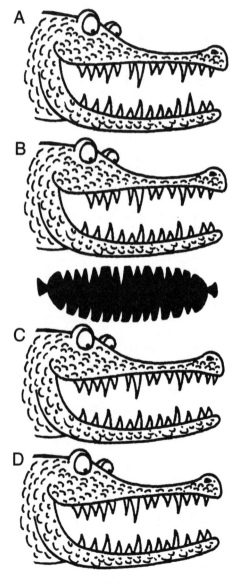

87. The Thirsty Biker

Which of the 4 paths will lead Gary to the lemonade?

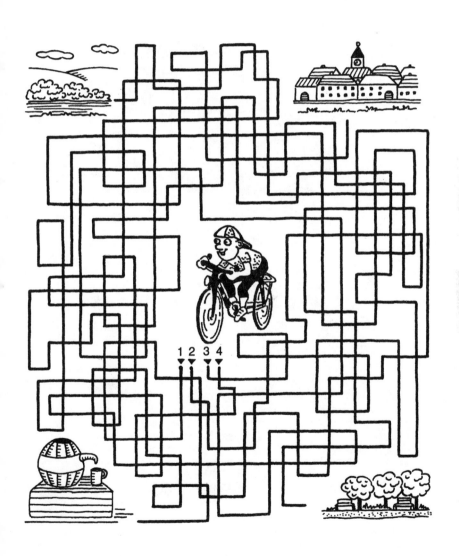

88. School Bus

Which of the 5 parts belongs to the bus?

89. Sorting Luggage

Which 6 pieces of luggage do not appear in both pictures?

90. Ear Science

Give every pair of ears to the right animal. When you do, there will be one pair of ears left. They belong to an animal that likes to see the world upside down. What is it called?

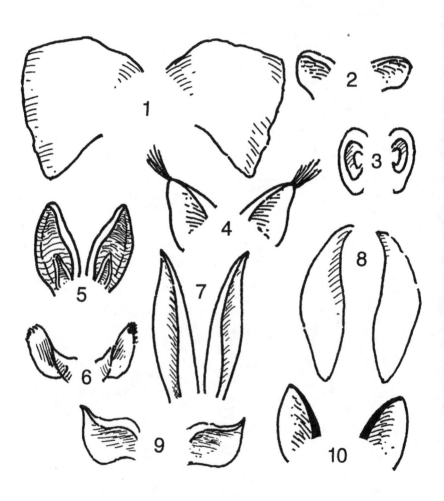

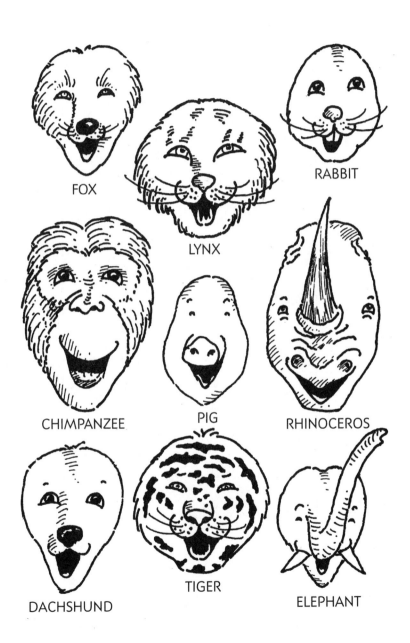

FOX

LYNX

RABBIT

CHIMPANZEE

PIG

RHINOCEROS

DACHSHUND

TIGER

ELEPHANT

103

91. Elephant Watch

Can you find 7 differences between the 2 pictures—before the commercial?

92. Tennis Lesson

When you connect the dots, you'll recognize the bear's opponent.

93. Who Won?

At the end of the soccer game, the field players of both teams decided to shoot at a goal at the same time. One team used only white balls, the other team only black balls. Even though all shots hit the goal, the only balls that count must add up to 50. So you need to find out how many balls of each color add up to exactly 50 points. Then you'll know who scored the most balls—and won!

94. Athletes

The picture at the top shows 11 athletes in action, and the bottom picture shows pieces of athletic equipment. What pairs belong together? Match up the letters and numbers. Who will be left without any equipment at all?

95. Number Spectacular

Add up all numbers and divide the sum by the number that occurs least! Multiply the result by the number that occurs most. (9 and 6 are not upside down.) What is the answer?

÷   =   X   =

96. Lone Fish

23 of the 24 fish in each aquarium appear in both tanks. But each tank has one loner. Can you find them?

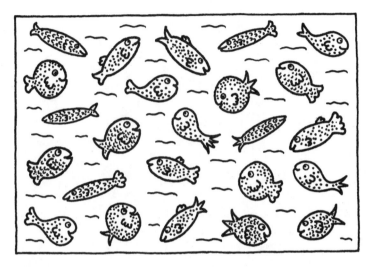

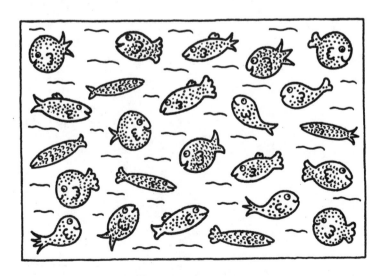

97. Fish Express

Connect the dots and you'll find out who is giving the fish a lift.

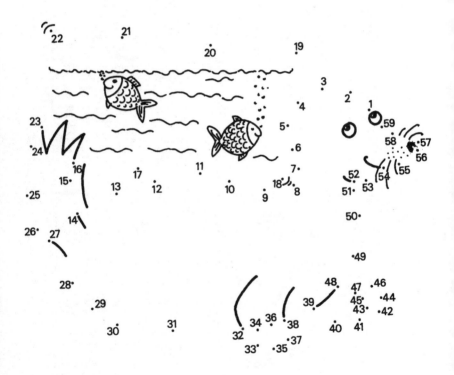

98. The Bird

What did the bird do most? Eat cherries—or sing songs?

99. Twins in the Pond

In the ponds below, 2 of the children are twins. And 2 of the ponds also look the same. Can you find the twin children—and the twin ponds?

6 TED

7 JACK

8 PAT

9 TONY

10 DAN

113

100. Who Lives Here?

Compare the shapes of the 6 dogs with the black drawing in the doghouse and you'll know who lives in it.

101. The Knight's Shield

Fill in the black areas needed on the shield of the knight at the bottom right, so that it follows the same kind of sequence as in the row above.

102. The Tower

This military tower was built from 11 of these 12 pieces. Look for the spots on the wall that match every piece exactly. Which piece is left over?

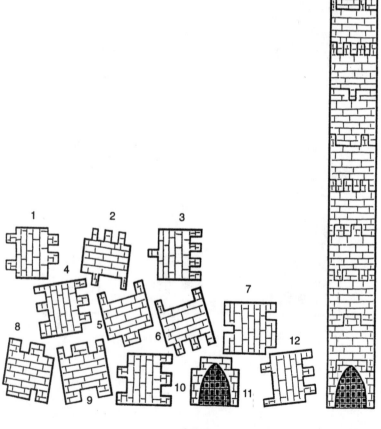

Answers

1. Swimming Marathon

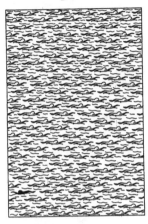

2. Down the Slide
The following children are triplets:

1, 18, 24   5, 19, 23
2, 10, 21   6, 8, 15
3, 7, 16   9, 13, 20
4, 12, 17   11, 14, 22

3. A Huge Hole
The moths ate 47 boxes.

4. Where Is My Wife?
She is #9.

5. Who Is Flying Where?
Plane 1: New York
Plane 2: Tunis
Plane 3: Helsinki

6. Long Tongues
The second from the bottom.

7. Looking for the Boomerang

8. Who Is Serving the Coffee?

9. On a Gondola in Venice
Canal #3.

10. Kite Festival
The kite with the triangular eyes is flying on the longest string.

11. Four Triplets
The triplets are: 3, 12, 15; 4, 6, 20; 2, 11, 17; and 7, 9, 14.

117

12. Camels

13. Wild River

14. Half a Crown
#4 will do it.

15. New Eyeglasses
#14 and 15.

16. Hat Heaven

17. Wash Day

18. Mysterious Request
House #5.

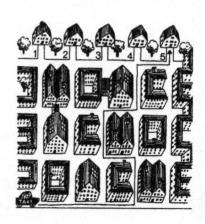

19. Rock Climbing

20. Greetings from the Woodchuck
#8.

21. Where is the 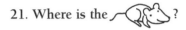 ?

22. How Old Is This Tree?
$2 + 5 + 9 + 11 + 13 = 40$
The tree is 40 years old.

23. Which 6 objects do not appear twice?
Folder, ear of corn, jug, wine glass, potato, walking stick.

24. Hibernation
Bear #5.

25. Gathering of the Ravens

26. In the Hat Shop
Picture on top: Billy takes the hat that is third from the left in the bottom row.
Picture below: The fourth hat from the left in the top row is the one that the clerk brought out of the back room to fill the hat stand.

27. Looking for Footprints

28. Home of the Fountain Pen
Case d.

29. Crazy about Bookmarks
Top book: The sixth page from the top.
Book in the middle: The sixth page from the bottom.
Bottom book: The fourth page from the bottom.

30. Gingerbread Dominoes
Charlie will be allowed to eat gingerbread #2/4.
It will work like this: 6/6 - 6/5 - 5/0 - 0/2 - 2/3 - 3/4 - 4/1 - 1/6.
Or like this: 6/6 - 6/1 - 1/4 - 4/3 - 3/2 - 2/0 - 0/5 - 5/6.

31. Many Great-Smelling Gingerbreads

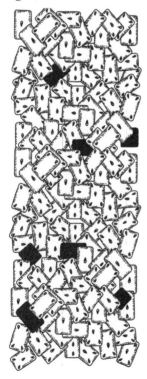

32. Hidden Gifts
Presents in pile #3.

33. From Fall to Winter
2 - 3 - 6 - 1 - 4; picture 5 does not fit, because swallows spend the winter in the south.

34. Star Points
Monica made the star with the fewest points (seventh from left, with only 4 points) and Mark made the star with the most points (third down from the top, with 8 points).

35. Where Is the Reindeer?

36. Self Service
A/3; B/5; C/1; D/2; E/4

37. Decorating the Christmas Tree
Balthasar, one of the Three Magi.

38. The Snowman's Hat
Pot #7.

39. A Sweet Job
The cookies with the numbers 9, 11, 20, 24, and 36 add up to 100.

40. Cookie Dough
Dough #3.

41. John's Christmas Wish
Guitar #8.

42. Amazing Violins

43. The Yawning Frog

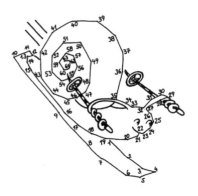

44. The Leaping Seal
Seal #5.

45. Four Skaters
The penguin on the left and one on the right at the top.

46. Skating Elks

47. Identical Squares
Beginning with the hockey-playing snowman:
A/4 – B/1;
F/2 – C/4;
H/1 – D/7.

48. The Sled

49. Tree Slalom
The second runner from the left is the only one to ski the course without mistakes.

50. Who Shot the Goal?
Jim.

51. What's the Game?

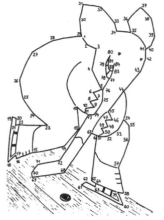

52. The Big Snowball Fight
Greg fights with Alice, Peter with Hannah, Eve with Will, Bob with Paul, Susanne with Ken, George with Philip.

53. Downhill Skiers

54. Let's Hit the Slopes

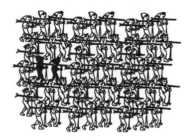

55. Six Snowballs
In the top snowball.

56. Snowman Mountain
You can build only five snowmen, because there are only five pots.

57. On the Track

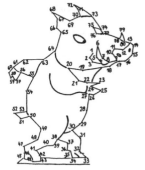

58. Bank Robbery

59. Potato Stamp
On paper #4.

60. Carnival Game
There are several possible solutions. One of them: Throw the ball into holes 8, 12, 17 and 23.

61. RRRRocket
Venus.

62. Lucky Hit
Hal.

63. On Top of the World

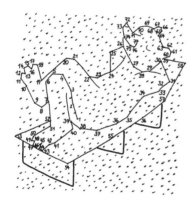

64. The Jester's Hat
Decoration #4.

65. Where Is My Mask?
Mask #8.

66. Calculating with 2 Clowns
The clown on top attended 77 costume parties, while the clown on the bottom attended 85.

67. Russian Doll

68 Three Faces....

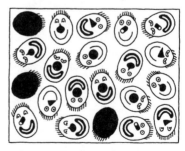

69. Butterflies
Butterfly #4.

123

70. Through the Hedge

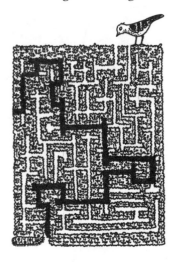

71. The Centipede

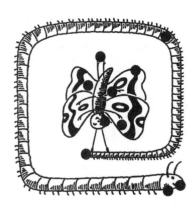

74. Where are the rabbits.?

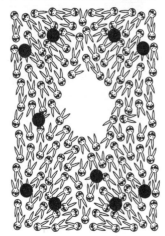

75. Painter and Model

76. Look for 15 differences!

72. Egg Fraud
Snail, turtle, crocodile.

73. Rabbit Company
Rabbit # 6.

77. A Museum Piece
The vase is 92 years old.

78. Painting Easter Eggs

Vickie 5	Jeff 3
David 3	Paula 1

79. The Giant Egg

80. Frog Tuba
Mouthpiece #2.

81. Who Is Riding?

82. Exchanging Ears
A/5; B/7; C/1; D/3; E/9; F/6;
G/4; H/2; I/8.

83. Who Is Older?
The engine on top is 62 and the
one on the bottom is 59 years
old.

84. Going Swimming
Picture #5.

85. Crocodile in Love
The fifth crocodile from the top.

86. Crocodile Snacks
Crocodile D.

87. The Thirsty Biker
Path #2.

88. School Bus
Part 4.

89. Which 6 pieces...

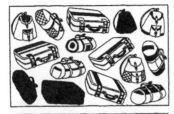

90. Ear Science
1. Elephant 2. Tiger
3. Chimpanzee, 4. Lynx.
6. Rhinoceros. 7. Rabbit.
8. Dachshund. 9. Pig. 10. Fox.
Ear-pair #5 is left, and it
belongs to a bat.

91. Elephant Watch

92. Tennis Lesson

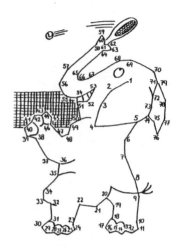

93. Who Won?
The team with the black balls
won. It took five balls (4 + 6 +
9 + 15 + 16) to add up to 50.
The team with the white balls
needed four balls for that (10 +
11 + 14 + 15).

94. Athletes
A/9; B/2; C/8; D/4; E/7; F/3;
G/10; H/1; J/6; K/5.
The golfer is the only one left
with no equipment.

95. Number Spectacular
90 divided by 6 = 15; 15 × 3 =
45.

96. Lone Fish

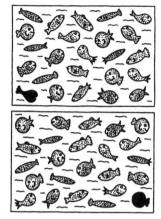

97. Fish Express

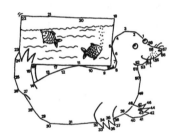

98. The Bird
The bird ate 62 cherries, but sang only 61 songs.

99. Twins in the Pond
Mary and Pat are twins, and ponds 2 and 10 are identical.

100. Who Lives Here?
Dog #3 lives in the doghouse.

101. The Knight's Shield

102. The Tower
Piece #6 is left over.

Index

128